I0791197

CLIMATE CHANGE AND ITS ROLE IN FORMING THE INSIDIOUS RELATIONSHIP BETWEEN NATURAL DISASTERS AND SOCIAL DISORDERS WITH A PREDICTION FOR THE FUTURE

DAVID REILLY

CLIMATE CHANGE AND ITS ROLE IN FORMING
THE INSIDIOUS RELATIONSHIP BETWEEN
NATURAL DISASTERS AND SOCIAL DISORDERS
WITH A PREDICTION FOR THE FUTURE

iUniverse books may be ordered through booksellers or by contacting:

iUniverse
1663 Liberty Drive
Bloomington, IN 47403
www.iuniverse.com
844-349-9409

*Because of the dynamic nature of the Internet, any web addresses or
links contained in this book may have changed since publication and
may no longer be valid. The views expressed in this work are solely those
of the author and do not necessarily reflect the views of the publisher,
and the publisher hereby disclaims any responsibility for them.*

*Any people depicted in stock imagery provided by Getty Images are
models, and such images are being used for illustrative purposes only.
Certain stock imagery © Getty Images.*

ISBN: 978-1-6632-4230-3 (sc)
ISBN: 978-1-6632-4229-7 (e)

Library of Congress Control Number: 2022912812

Print information available on the last page.

iUniverse rev. date: 08/11/2022

CONTENTS

CHAPTER 1

INTRODUCTION

This book has its genesis in two sources of lack of understanding. The first concerns the cascading increase of natural disasters afflicting the world, which were seemingly more frequent, intense, and widespread in America, although that is, perhaps, a function of living there. The second concerns the increase in the frequency, intensity, numbers, and vicious nature of social disruptions and disorders that have been taking place across the country, particularly among the younger population.

As a psychologist with many years of experience dealing with various types of psychopathologies, I was struck by the seemingly random nature of the increase in social disorders and violence. The increase seemed to coincide with the cascading increase in natural disasters but was there a causal relationship?

The increase in the onslaught of natural disasters, along with a disturbing rise in various types of significant social disruptions, each with long-lasting effects requiring substantial changes in both physical and social aspects of

American life, require review of a serious nature by experts. Could the type, extent, or nature of natural disasters visited upon the country be related to the increased spawning of social disorders? If so, how can this be documented?

It is far beyond the scope of this book to identify all of the factors that suggest this hypothesis is valid. It is not beyond the book's capacity to paint enough of a picture for experts in each of these areas to consider the available data and come to a serious and definite conclusion. However, the currently available data are neither specific nor sufficient for the research that needs undertaking before a researcher can venture a valid answer.

This book does not intend to cover all aspects and variables that influence these issues. Such critical issues as climate refugees, financial incentives, putting off having children, and many others are not discussed here.

Hopefully, the purpose is to alert and reinforce among people of all countries that the dangers from natural disasters and social disorders, each by itself, are genuine. If, however, they are combined in their formation and effects with other natural disasters or inter-related with social conditions, the dangers are magnified several times over.

The short answer to the question "could they be they related" appears to be "yes. The answer indeed seems valid in a correlational sense. But correlation does not imply or describe a causative relationship, as any first-year course in statistics makes clear.

This is not just an academic question. Suppose natural disasters are not causally related to an increase in social disorders. In that case, each must be dealt with separately, but hopefully concurrently. If their occurrences are causally related, then totally different and probably much more complex and complicated responses will be required to resolve them.

This book addresses this question but does not provide an absolute answer to it. The data necessary for doing so are lacking. Hopefully, however, the book does provide sufficient information to alert others to a potential natural disaster-social disorder relationship with promising research avenues to be explored by others from a variety of disciplines.

CHAPTER 2

OVERVIEW

Humankind has always been subject to natural disasters. Records from long ago make it clear that floods, famines, and plagues of all kinds, caused severe damage to physical structures, often with a significant loss of life. These effects also caused mental and emotional traumas that resulted in powerful feelings of guilt for having displeased whatever gods may have been in vogue at the time. These feelings often resulted in sacrifices of animals, the cream of the population, or captured enemies to regain favor with the gods. In the direst of circumstances, a sacrifice of adolescents, males, but primarily females, would be made.

These can be considered the first cases of social disorders attributable to the impact of natural disasters. The primary mechanism operating was a projection of anger towards others that behavioral outbursts, including sacrifices, were thought able to salve. Anything that threatened to remove control or independence was to be rejected or done away with. Thus, blame for the disaster and its aftermath resulted from others' behavior, and no guilt needed to be internalized.

Many of the social disorders seen in the past months can be considered modern-day exercises of the same type of projection, with similar psycho-dynamics, as operated long ago. They both originated from natural disasters underlying their causation. Today's disorders are generated by impulsive behavior, emotional responses to perceived insults, or intrusions of personal space. Lethal firearms accompany these, and a variety of social discriminations, faster travel, and seemingly under-qualified political leaders and media coverage provide little leadership and understanding of the unfolding events.

Little attention has been paid to one of the most potent motivators of this social disorder behavior. Suppose more attention had been given to this factor by the general public. In that case, understanding one of the consequences of natural disasters is a loss of security and well-being would be prevalent. Often accompanying these feelings are a lack of control over one's life and destiny and a fear of feeling helpless. In many households, it is a feeling of being unable to provide for one's family.

These feelings can easily lead to PTSD. Evading feelings of loss of security and well-being are significant aspects of leading a happy, healthy life. Having these torn out from under you, often without any warning, can lead to substantial personal and social problems. The length of the recovery period from PTSD can vary from short-term to years. As will be discussed further in the book, these feelings of lack of control over one's life are manifested in a variety of behavioral outbursts that are often hurtful to others and oneself.

The plan of this book is quite simple. First, an examination of natural disasters (NDs), their type, frequency, intensity, and growth are provided and discussed. The author has also offered problems with the current method of listing NDs.

A model for cataloging NDs by type, severity, etc., will also be presented. Second, a discourse on social disorder and disruption will be presented, followed by a chapter discussing possible causes, manifestations, and dynamics that could give rise to the disorders. The next chapter begins with a change of perspective necessary to understand the system interactions that are the core of the problem.

The reader should note that the government and its agencies have not been absent from ameliorating the effects of various disasters. For example, FEMA has calculated the frequency of natural disaster declarations during the past five years. This data resulted in the following percentage for each of the indicated disasters.

- Wildfires/fires—44%
- Severe storms/flooding—26%
- Tropical storm or hurricane—11%
- Severe Winter storm—10%
- Tornados—8%
- Earthquakes—1%

Knowing this data and assuming the future effects of climate change do not significantly alter the disaster list or percentages provides valuable information for pre-event planning.

Likewise, in 2007 (Volume 13, No.1-January), the CDC issued a report dealing with epidemics after natural disasters. Their data also indicates what planning efforts should be established as priorities for post-event needs. Unfortunately, these data do not include provision for any cascading of disasters when two or more coincide, or are in close time proximity (Reilly, to be published 2022).

CHAPTER 3

UNDERSTANDING NATURAL DISASTERS - LINEAR, NON-LINEAR, OR BOTH?

A major flaw in investigating natural disasters, and especially ways in which they may be related to social disorders, has been examining each in isolation from other disasters. This is essentially a reductionist methodology that can shed light on the specific disaster but does not allow the interrelationships among disasters and their connections to social disorders to be considered.

It is abundantly clear that a linear relationship does not exist with respect to natural disasters. They are non-linear in process, and a non-linear perspective is necessary to understand the complexity of the relationships within natural disasters and their connections with social disorders.

The Table below describes five of the critical differences between linear and non-linear processes and systems.

CRITICAL DIFFERENCES BETWEEN LINEAR AND NON-LINEAR SYSTEMS		
	Linear	Non-linear
Initial Conditions	Not Important	Critical
Equilibrium	Stability	Chaos
Prediction	Deterministic	Chance
Feedback	Negative	Positive
Philosophy	Reductionism	Expansion

There are three critical characteristics of non-linear systems. These are:

- Irregular periodicity,
- Sensitivity to initial conditions and minute changes in the process, and
- Lack of predictability.

Each of the five differences noted above is critical for understanding and predicting the behavior of a non-linear system (NLS). The concept of the dimension of initial conditions (often called the butterfly effect) is absolutely critical. It is important to remember that minor initial differences can have profound effects on later system behavior. Using wildfires as an example, slight differences in the amount of combustible underbrush can mean the difference between a manageable or out-of-control wildfire.

A second difference is the concept of equilibrium. In

linear systems, the behavior of the system is oriented towards maintaining or re-establishing the stability of the system if there has been a disruption of the system's functioning.

In NLS, the disruption of the system (discussed below) is driven by positive feedback. This leads to irregular behavior patterns. The discrepancy between the initial conditions and the current ones accentuates the differences, often leading to a state of chaos in the system's behavior. It can also result in a re-organization of the system into a more complex form, hopefully leading to a more stable state.

In linear systems, prediction is deterministic. In NLS results occur by chance and are not predictable. However, it is possible to approach a valid prediction of future system behavior. This prediction depends on being able to identify critical variables in a quantifiable form. A form of a Basic Logistic Equation (Malthusian Version) will be discussed in the next section. Hopefully, it will lead to the development of an equation that analyses natural disaster formation and relations and is able to predict social disorder development.

Feedback in linear systems serves to alert the system that established boundaries of the system have been reached or breached. This alerts the system that self-corrective action must be taken to re-establish the stability of the system.

In non-linear systems, feedback is positive and serves to actuate the difference between an initial condition and a resulting one. This, in turn, serves to increase the chaotic condition of the system.

The last difference between linear and non-linear systems is the philosophical base of each. In a linear system, the base is reductionism. That is, systems, whether physical, behavioral, or other can best be understood by reducing the phenomenon under scrutiny to its lowest element and studying it in minute detail. This process serves well the search in a physical or biological system when seeking the virus responsible for the latest epidemic.

In non-linear systems, the base is creativity and expansion. This means the system is best understood in terms of the inter-relationships among its various components. In fact, it can only be understood in terms of these relationships, for it is the interactions that give the system definition and meaning. By isolating one component of the study to study in detail, the relationships among components are lost, as are the meaning and understanding of the system.

Natural disasters are subject to each of these characteristics, and other variables. It is also a valid perception that various types of disasters will demonstrate varying degrees of susceptibility for each of these characteristics. Every kind of natural disaster will need to be studied with non-linear concepts in mind in order to understand its relationships sufficiently to apply a non-linear equation to it for estimating future changes as the disaster unfolds.

It is essential to apply these five considerations to natural disasters at two levels. The first is to each disaster in and of itself.

The second is to add each succeeding disaster of the same type to the first and then each succeeding one in its turn. This action will provide an increasing set of inter-actions to examine. By examining them as a large complex set of systems, understandings and insights may emerge that would not be apparent by examining only one disaster separate from others.

It is this combination of linear and non-linear processes

that makes the relationships between natural disasters and social disorders so insidious to decipher and understand. Each category, disaster, and disorder, are huge spheres touching and interacting with each other. Inside each is other spheres that interact with each other. Each sphere must be deciphered and quantified. Then, we will be in a position to begin understanding how together they can be predicted to result in the outcomes we tend to think of as separate.

Pattern Recognition and Integration

Non-linear systems theory has been used to describe patterns in physical and social sciences. Formulas have been developed to describe these patterns. An equation frequently used to predict the annual population of fish in a pond is shown in the following figure.

Basic Logistic Difference Equation (Malthusian Version)

$Xnext + rx(1-x)$
Where:
x= A chosen starting value
r=a rate of growth that can be set higher or lower
(1-x) a term to keep the growth within limits
Example: xnext =2.5 (.001) (1-.001)

In order to identify patterns and interpret them, it is first necessary to identify the critical variables. These will vary from one type of disaster to another. Thus, it is essential to quantify each variable to be compared on such variables as intensity, frequency, damage potential, likely changes of direction, and overall costs, among others. A primary goal would be to understand them sufficiently (a combination of reductionism and expansionism would be necessary) to allow predictions of social disorders arising from types of NDs and their characteristics.

The author has used the formula indicated to forecast the learning levels of students while using four variables. These were the initial level of knowledge, student learning effectiveness, teacher effectiveness, and rate of instruction. (Reilly, 1998)

By holding three variables constant and varying one, the changes in learning effectiveness due to one variable's changes can be ascertained. A similar process should yield an essential understanding of disaster variables and the extent of each disaster. When such data are extracted from several similar disasters, researchers will have far more extensive knowledge of the disasters and their interactions. This understanding should lead to valid predictive models.

Unfortunately, the number, intensity, and damaging effects of natural disasters in the US seem similar to the increase in disasters in other countries. They last longer and inflict increasing amounts of damage on individuals, physical structures, coastlines, and many other natural resources and many people's psyches. A planet-wide perspective must be developed as a means for implementing corrective measures assured on a planet-wide basis.

Future conceptual models of natural disasters and predicting their effects must include linear and non-linear principles in their formations. Equally, these models must incorporate a planet-wide perspective in their construction. This is truly a formidable task requiring the best of the best in the attempt to identify the critical variables involved in understanding climate change, its component processes and elements, and their relationship to social disorders.

CHAPTER 4

TYPES OF NATURAL DISASTERS

Natural disasters are nothing new to humans. Almost all ancient writings refer to natural disasters of one sort or another. They did not, however, report planet-wide disasters. This lack of a report may be because there not being any, or more likely, there were no humans who could report such events.

Climate change, despite what the naysayers for whatever mystical reasons, want us to believe that it is not an actual and dangerous process that is occurring. They could not be more wrong. Any number of data sets supports the understanding that climate change is a natural, uncontrolled set of planet-wide processes. It affects any number of environmental and social functions. Sarah Gibbens, among many others, has been tracking the effects of climate change in very inhospitable locations.

In the September 2021 issue of <u>National Geographic</u>, she reports on changes that have taken place high in the Andes (19,000 feet). There has been significant depletion in the watershed, glaciers, and snow cover. These losses have their highest impact on the rivers of the area, an important factor to keep in mind. That is, one element of change often leads to others that have far more reaching and serious outcomes.

According to Gino Casassa, head of the Chilean government's glacier unit, conditions are approaching a mega-drought. Because these losses occur at such high altitudes, towns, farmers, and others far downstream can feel the effects, and the water towers are in danger from climate change. This water problem is also a problem for areas in the Himalayas.

The naysayers are wrong when they deny the existence of planet-wide changes that are a function of climate change. The naysayers deny the severe nature of this process, not only from the primary natural disasters but also from the secondary effects of these disasters.

For example, on the topic of climate and mass migrations:

"We've seen big shifts in how water moves around the planet because warm air holds more water vapor than cold. As a result, we see big increases in drought in dry areas and with it these massive and wicked wildfires. And then we see big increases in precipitation, downpour, and flood in wet areas. And all those things are combining already to produce high human costs. These include the early stages of what most people predict will be by far the biggest migrations in human history as people flee places that have simply become too hot or too salty or too flooded or too dry to allow them to go on living there. And I don't need to tell you what the national security, international security implications of that many people on the move will be." (Turrentine, 2019)

Climate change encompasses the entire planet. It can begin a process in one sector of the world, which causes disasters in another area. According to a report by Llan Kelman, writing in the Washington Post on July 7, 2021, he reported that floods were sweeping through villages in Germany and wholly engulfing subway stations in China. These floods in Germany were deemed nine times more likely because of climate change. A town was scorched to ruins in British Columbia while hundreds were dying in triple-digit heat in the Pacific Northwest. Tennessee recorded record floods with a high number of deaths.

NATURAL DISASTERS

STRESS LEVEL (PRE-DISASTER)

(level varies by interaction of type, intensity, personal and environmental factors

PERSONAL DISORDERS

(Increased stress, job loss, time factor)

MAY LEAD TO

Sense of loss of control over life)

MAY LEAD T0
Anti Social Disorders and/or Social Disorders
Fueled by

Depression Denial	Domestic Violence	Projection of blame on others
Drinking	Underlying prejudice	Drive-by shootings

In the past 700 years, China has suffered the most in the number of NDs and citizens killed. China is prone to several natural disasters such as flooding, droughts, earthquakes, typhoons, and more. Some of the worst natural disasters of all time have occurred in China and some of the world's most expensive disasters, such as the 1998 Yangtze River floods.

These floods and earthquakes, combined with the droughts and famines it has experienced, make China a leading candidate for the world's most disaster-prone country. Even so, it has not experienced many of the types of NDs that afflict other countries.

Each country or section of the world seems to experience more of one kind than others. Around the Pacific Rim, for example, earthquakes seem more prevalent. However, these often result in tsunamis that are a product of underwater earthquakes. And in the southern regions, hurricanes, cyclones, and typhoons seem to be just as dangerous.

As dangerous as each is, these disasters are not the worst or most serious that the contemporary planet has to fear. The ones facing Earth currently and for the foreseeable future are without previous occurrences, at least in human memory. They involve disasters that can engulf the entire land mass and much of the Earth's oceans. Indeed, as we have recently seen, viruses have this capability. We are being warned that even more deadly ones seem likely in the future.

In addition to the viruses, there is a strong likelihood of significant flooding over the next 20 years. This flooding will encompass considerable portions of low-lying lands, islands, cities, and harbors and submerge large areas of arable land in current farmlands. Even now, examples of what lies ahead are evident in the USA. Across the Eastern seaboard, thousands of trees have succumbed to the encroaching salt water reaching their habitat, and homes are being swept out to sea. And Washington, D.C., has experienced heavier flooding from storms and tides that are creeping in from rising seawater (www.nbcwashington.com/weather)

At the same time, significantly higher than normal tides, combined with strong storms, inundated the streets of Charleston, SC, with flood effects down to Savannah, GA.

During the summer of 2021, Europe, especially Germany and Belgium, suffered flooding of catastrophic proportions. Over 180 people had been confirmed as dead, and many more were still missing at the time of this writing. Property losses and losses to infrastructure were roughly estimated to be in the high millions. Secondary effects can wreak almost as much damage as the actual event.

It does not take much imagination to picture what will happen if the next pandemic occurs during such planet-wide flooding. The question is whether humanity would cease to exist on Earth.

There are different ways of categorizing natural disasters. Each type demands a separate type of categorization. A standard method, for example, with a hurricane, is by measuring its effects by the number of people hurt or killed, the number forced to evict their homes, the cost to infrastructure and homes, and the total cost, as well as other factors. These items provide a format for obtaining a pretty good picture of the hurricane's effects. But it would be totally inappropriate for measuring the effects of a drought.

Another is to categorize the number and intensity of each hurricane and its speed.

Each of these provides valuable data, but the problem is that the data is captured only for the particular type of disaster with either method. If Hurricane B follows

Hurricane A after six weeks the data for that hurricane is recorded separately. At the same time, if wildfires are devastating forests, towns, homes, and the social structure associated with a particular area of the country, the fires tend to be recorded separately from the hurricanes.

Templates for recording disasters are not readily available. There are no criteria for specifying exactly where the impact of a particular disaster begins and ends, for example. Data for estimating costs are just estimates until years after the event in many cases. Data are gathered in many instances by different methods according to the state or agency responsible for collecting it. These loopholes should be addressed and resolved by FEMA.

Types of Natural Disasters

The number of types of natural disasters depends on what agency you look to for data. Several governmental and private agencies and organizations report various numbers. They don't even have to be primarily involved with natural disasters. Again, the number and type depend on the criteria used. These criteria often differ significantly. It is vitally important that these differences be addressed and resolved. Otherwise, any efforts to develop, research, and deal with NDs more effectively will be stymied by not having an agreed set of criteria to identify amounts and types of resources to deal with disasters.

The Robert Stafford Disaster Relief and Emergency Assistance Act was signed into law on November 23, 1988, and has been amended several times. It provides the statutory authority for most disaster response actions and establishes the presidential declaration process.

The Disaster Recovery Reform Act of 2018 (DRRA, Division D of P.L. 115-254) was enacted on October 5, 2018. It is supposed to be the most comprehensive reform of the Federal Emergency Management Agency's (FEMA's) disaster assistance programs since the passage of the Sandy Recovery Improvement Act of 2013 (SRIA, Division B of P.L. 113-2) and the post-Katrina recovery programs.

These two acts are typical of the government's response to disasters. They are enacted after a disaster, rather than anticipating types of disaster and allocating funds to prevent or ameliorate its effects in advance.

The cumulative costs of these disasters, excluding the deaths they have been responsible for, have been horrendous. Adam Smith is the lead scientist for NOAA National Centers for Environmental Information's (NCEI's) U.S. Billion-dollar Weather and Climate Disasters. On January 8, 2021, he reported that disasters during 2020 cost 22 billion dollars.

Definition of Natural Disaster

There is general agreement as to the definition of natural disasters. Wikipedia defines a natural disaster as

> "a major adverse event resulting from natural processes of the Earth; examples include floods, hurricanes, tornadoes, volcanic eruptions, earthquakes, tsunamis, storms, and other geologic processes." (www.wikipedia.org).

The Department of Homeland Security says,

> "Natural disasters include all types of severe weather, which have the potential to pose a significant threat to human health and safety, property, critical infrastructure, and homeland security." (www.dhs.gov/natural-disasters).

As general and vague as these definitions seem, they serve a purpose by allowing almost any type of non-human caused disaster to be included in its meaning. They do not provide the specificity necessary for a comprehensive analysis of the specific disaster or its relationships and interactive effects with other disasters.

Many of these disasters are specific to a particular country, state, region of Earth, or area of a specific portion of a nation. This myopic view of disasters is a significant impediment to developing a comprehensive understanding of the planet-wide interactive effects of natural disasters. Earth must be viewed as a whole if it is to remain habitable for humans.

For example, as <u>National Geographic</u> reported in its November 2021 edition (by Kieran Dodds), climate change is now having a disastrous effect on the Earth's polar regions. These effects include the loss of artifacts from prehistoric cultures and many from Alaska's shores and beyond.

As Dodds reports, coastal Alaska is being pummeled by a one-two punch of rising temperatures and rising seas. The ground is now thawed down to three feet compared to 18 inches about 12 years ago.

24 TYPES OF NATURAL DISASTER
AVALANCHE
HAILSTORM
ICE STORM
COLD WAVE
BLIZZARD
SOLAR FLARE
WILDFIRE
HEAT WAVE
DROUGHT
VOLCANIC ERUPTION
TORNADO
IMPACT EVENT
LIMNIC ERUPTION
TSUNAMI
THUNDERSTORM
TROPICAL CYCLONE
FLOOD
FLASH FLOOD
LANDSLIDE
EARTHQUAKE
SUBSIDENCE
MUDSLIDE
SINKHOLE
KILLER FOG
Outforia

In alphabetical order these are:

1. Avalanches
2. Blizzards
3. Cold Waves
4. Droughts
5. Earthquakes
6. Floods
7. Hail Storms
8. Hear Wave
9. Hurricanes
10. Ice Storms
11. Impact Event
12. Landslides
13. Limnic Eruption
14. Mudslide
15. Pea Soup Fog
16. Sinkholes
17. Solar Flares
18. Thunderstorms
19. Tornadoes
20. Tropic Cyclone
21. Virus
22. Volcanic Eruption
23. Wild Fires
24. Plague*
25. Famine*

* Added by the author. One of Pilson's 24, subsidence, was omitted because it was subsumed under flooding.

There are several records of NDs that have occurred over the past three centuries. Wikipedia has provided a significant contribution to a chronological list of natural disasters. These are listed by category of avalanches, earthquakes, fires, and others that provide a very useful historical perspective of each disaster type.

Our World in Data is another organization that provides a world of data on 19 different Indicators. Although not providing data specifically on types of NDs, it does provide helpful information on such Indicators as Disaster Risk, Biodiversity, Emissions, and Air Pollution, and one that will be very useful in the next section of this book on social disorders.

Outfornia, written by Gaby Pilson, who is an outdoor educator among other outdoor leadership activities, has developed a list of 24 types of natural disasters. As indicated in the Table below she has listed them according to the season of the year, and to some extent geographical region.

Pilson has done an excellent service by listing these disaster types and especially showing what geographical region they are most common. Certainly, inhabitants of the American Southeast would not be concerned about a snow avalanche. On the other hand, they would be most concerned with hurricanes, droughts, heat waves, and, more recently, flooding.

From planning and logistic points of view, these are essential elements for developing a broad-based plan for the future. Such planning efforts on a planet-wide basis are imperative.

Elizabeth Royte, writing in the July 2021 issue of the National Geographic, 40-65, has described the heat conditions in many of Earth's locations. She concluded that rising heat is likely to push millions of people and entire regions out of their temperature comfort zones if climate changes keep happening. Indeed, planning and acting now with this knowledge would be a significant help to the people affected.

There are, however, several difficulties involved in trying to classify, type, and specify natural disasters. There is any number of federal, state, and local agencies that have responsibility for recording the number of natural disasters. Some associations and organizations collect similar data.

The discrepancies among these different groups can be significant.

There needs to be agreement on what constitutes a natural disaster and each type of disaster. A good starting point would be each of the 24 listed previously. With the lack of agreed-upon definitions and parameters for each type of disaster, there can be no meaningful data extracted to provide baseline and follow-up data. The first step would be to establish a national council to develop and publish agreed-upon definitions and parameters for each type of disaster. This council should be initiated by FEMA, although not necessarily respond to it. Any efforts by political leaders to modify these disaster definitions should be reported and resisted.

CHAPTER 5

EFFECTS OF NATURAL DISASTERS AND SPIN-OFF EFFECTS

Natural Disasters by Type and Level

Three levels of natural disasters will be discussed in this chapter. Level 1 disasters are more frequent and generally, more severe than Level 2 disasters. That is not to say that Level 2 disasters are not to be worried about. They should be, but they are less frequently encountered. The spin-off effects of each disaster are often, if not more, dangerous than the disaster itself. They can last for years as in re-building after a hurricane. The financial impact can run into the billions. And the personal losses of homes, and jobs can place an extremely heavy stress burden on many. The less economically advantaged are usually hurt most by disasters. Level 3 disasters are rare and not discussed here.

The disasters listed below are not in any particular order. Readers should, however, be mindful of those that are more frequent in the area of the country where they live.

Level 1 Disasters

There is any number of types of disasters but without an accepted definition of a natural disaster and its level of severity, accurate numbers and data are not possible. The disasters discussed here are ones that most reasonable individuals would consider as a very serious level of disaster,

Droughts

Primary Effects

A drought is an event of prolonged shortages in water or groundwater. A drought can last for months or years or be declared after as few as 15 days. It can substantially impact the ecosystem and agriculture of the affected region and harm the local economy.

Although seemingly not recognized by many in the USA, drought conditions have reached a dangerously low level in the Western portions. For example, the Western megadrought is so bad water has to be airlifted to animals. The first water cuts ever had to be made from the Colorado River, probably water cuts for Arizona and Nevada.

In another area of the planet, the Middle East is running out of water, and in Africa a walk of several miles for a bucket of water us not uncommon.

Annual dry seasons in the tropics significantly increase the chances of a drought developing and subsequent bush fires. Periods of heat can significantly worsen drought conditions by hastening the evaporation of water vapor.

Profound, prolonged droughts in America, Africa,

Portions of South America, Iraq, and other middle east countries are of current concern.

One of the difficulties in trying to understand droughts is that several agencies categorize droughts on different scales. For example, the Palmer Drought Index, the CPC Soil Moisture Model, and the National Weather Service use other models to determine the severity of a drought. And the number of categories of drought conditions differ, as do the ways of measuring the severity.

Droughts do not arise overnight. It can take years before the total damage from a lack is apparent. There is a giant aquifer in the Southwest of America that many wells have tapped for many years. It has about reached its limit.

This lack of water takes a severe toll on humans and animals alike. Humans have more flexibility in how they respond. Animals have no such reserves. In the most brutal and prolonged droughts, humans must decide between poor choices, sell their animals, slaughter them, or try to save a few. In any of these options, humans will lose much of their income.

If humans had crops instead of animals, the results would be about the same. As the crops wither and die, the following year's seed money dies with the crops. After two or three years of prolonged drought, the land will fallow.

Rod Nickel and Tom Polansek, reporting for Reuters, (Sept. 3, 2021) interviewed several ranchers in Manitoba, Canada. One of the ranchers they interviewed was Dianne Riding.

Record-setting heat and light rain left Riding with too little grass or hay to feed her cattle near Lake Francis, Manitoba. She sold 51 head of cattle at auction in July, about

40% of her herd. The sales included 20 heifers, young cows that had not given birth, and potential breeding stock.

"That's your future. As my herd goes down, so does my income," Riding said. "It's gut-wrenching."

According to two dozen ranchers and cattle experts, such liquidations of breeding stock are expected to limit cattle production in the coming years. This will reduce North America's beef supply and drive-up consumer prices.

The drought spanning much of western North America - from Canada to California and Mexico - has cooked pastures and hay crops that fatten cattle. The ranchers' plight is one impact of many of the punishing effects of the drought. This has also damaged wheat across North Dakota and cherries in Washington; weakened bee colonies, and forced California to shut down a primary hydroelectric plant. In British Columbia, an entire town burned. At the same time, California expects to see a record number of acres go up in flames this year.

Climate scientists say global warming makes extreme heat and drought occur more frequently. However, some ranchers interviewed by Reuters dispute the link to climate change. They view the current drought as an unremarkable shift in the weather from which the industry will recover.

Riding said she is tired of scientists blaming agriculture, among other industries, for climate-warming greenhouse gas emissions. "I know climate change is our latest buzzword, but I think this is a cycle," said Riding, 60, whose farm northwest of Winnipeg sits in one of the hardest-hit drought areas. "Sometimes, the cycles are longer than normal."

Gloria Montaño Greene, Deputy Under Secretary for Farm Production and Conservation (FPAC) a U.S. who works to reduce risks to farming, said the connection between the West Coast drought and climate change is clear. "There is an increase in heat, and we see various wildfires," she said. "We're seeing climate change."

Adding to ranchers' problems, feed alternatives such as corn, soy, and wheat are the highest in years. There is so little feed available that Manitoba farmers have bought 280 tons of hay from as far away as Prince Edward Island, some 3,400 km (2,000 miles) to the east.

In a typical year, 10% to 12% of breeding stock in western Canada, the country's top beef-producing region, are culled due to age or other routine reasons. Farmers replace most of it, said Brian Perillat, senior analyst at CanFax.

In 2021 ranchers are likely to cull 20% to 30%, reducing the size of herds, according to the industry group Alberta Beef Producers. That would be an unprecedented reduction of the breeding stock, based on records going back to 1970, Perillat said.

Analysts expect a more negligible impact in the United States, the world's third-biggest beef exporter because the herd is more spread out. Still, a third of U.S. cattle are in drought areas, according to the U.S. Drought Monitor, and producers are making the painful decision to send animals to slaughter early. New Mexico rancher Pat Boone, 67, slashed his herd of mother cows by half, to about 200 head, over the past year. "Our land is hurt, and it's hurt badly," said Boone, who lives in Elida, a town of about 200 people in eastern New Mexico. "We're not going to be in any hurry to restock."

Fewer Cows Leads to Higher Beef Prices

Sending female cows to slaughter in 2021, instead of keeping them for breeding, will reduce market-ready cattle inventories in 2023, economists say. The animals have long gestation periods and take time to fatten after birth.

"When we liquidate cow herds, these supply impacts last years," said Mike von Massow, associate professor of food, agricultural, and resource economics at the University of Guelph, Ontario. "You have this hangover."

In a recent earnings report, Tyson Foods, the biggest U.S. meat company by sales, expects operating margins for its booming beef business to decline next year amid herd liquidation. Its results should still be strong.

Riding says she will need four years to rebuild her herd. If the drought abates, she might retain or buy heifers next year. But the animals don't produce their first calf until they turn two years old.

Consumers will also feel the pinch, analysts said. The USDA in August trimmed its estimates for U.S. beef production this year and next as ranchers are raising animals to lighter weights.

After a 2014 drought, beef prices in Canada rose about 25% over the following year and stayed elevated for at least two years, von Massow said, citing Statistics Canada data. He said that beef prices are likely to increase as early as this fall, reflecting the higher prices to feed cattle.

In Mexico, the northern state of Chihuahua has gone from around 1.2 million breeding cows in 2019 to about 700,000 because of drought, according to Fernando Cadena, head of Mexican ranching company Carnes Ribe based in Ciudad de Chihuahua, just south of Texas.

Cadena reported other central northern Mexican ranching states like Sonora, Coahuila, Nuevo Leon, and Durango, saw similar rates of drought-induced slaughter. These were in addition to cows that died on parched land due to lack of food or water.

He said the hardest hit ranchers in northern Mexico would likely need two to four years to recover herd levels.

Fewer cows in Mexico could impact the U.S. beef supply, as more than a million cows are imported across the southern border each year. "We'll just have to wait for the pasture land to recover," Cadena said. "For months, it just didn't rain. There wasn't anywhere for the cows to graze."

Feedlots, which buy cattle from ranchers and fatten them for slaughter, are also worried about their businesses. Greg Schmidt, who feeds 15,000 cattle near Barrhead, Alberta, expects to pay more for available cattle next year after herds are reduced.

"This is going to ripple through our industry for years," said Schmidt, chair of the Alberta Cattle Feeders' Association.

All of these changing conditions with their attendant losses increase the stress level further by future projections of losses and loss of family operations.

Ponds Turned to Dry Earth

The United States Drought Monitor is produced by a rotating group of authors and incorporates reviews from a group of 250 climatologists, extension agents, and others across the nation. It also incorporates the views of those being affected by drought conditions. Each week the authors revise the previous map based on rainfall, snowfall, and other events, and observers' reports of how drought is affecting crops, wildlife, and other indicators

A rancher in Pozo, California, Steve Arnold, said 12 of the last 15 years had brought less than half of average rainfall to his area about 200 miles northwest of Los Angeles. But Arnold, 67, said this drought is the worst he has seen. Grass never grew this year due to the lack of rainfall. He has reduced his herd by about 30% to about 70 head. "We've had dry stuff but not like this," he said.

Tony Toso, 58, who raises cows and calves in the foothills of the Sierra Nevada mountains, said that ponds that used to provide drinking water for cattle are dried up in parts of California.

"I'm seeing ponds that usually may get low, but not where they're cracked dirt," said Toso, president of the California Cattlemen's Association. "There's nothing in them."

With grass in short supply, Toso expects prices for alfalfa hay to top $300 per ton, up from $200 to $220 per ton last year. The rancher said he did not retain any calves to replace his herd of mother cows as he usually would because of the drought and outlook for little feed. Instead, the animals all went to the market to be slaughtered for beef.

The land will need to be sold, probably at a lower price than it is worth. The farmers will likely have to move, and if they are lucky, they will be able to obtain a job that allows them and their families to continue existing.

In Africa, the drought is severe and affects millions of people. Combined with the famine that covers much of the continent it is estimated that 20 million people, many of them children, are at high risk of starving.

Spin-off Effects

A significant spin-off effect is the probability of flooding. The flooding is an instance of the impact of climate change, notably the increase in temperature worldwide. Loss of jobs, land, and income are all possible.

Famine

Famines are the running mates of droughts. If the drought persists long enough, a famine will emerge unless one of two conditions is present. The first is an adequate supply of water from a river. If the drought continues and there is a heavy demand on the river(s) for a sustained amount of time, it is possible for the river to run dry or for the amount of water taken from it to be cut. This situation pervades the American Southwest, where the aquifer feeding the area (a vast area) for people, crops, drilling needs, and animals has been drained almost to the point of exhaustion. The lakes that fed it have reached historic lows. The Colorado River, for the first time, will have the amount of water taken from it cut.

The second condition is if a prolonged period of rain increases the water flow from lakes. Relying on this to occur is an iffy proposition and not a dependable one.

It is not just in the USA that famine has raised its dangerous head. In fact, in some countries, its whole body is exposed and has been for some time. Currently, the Sudan and Madagascar are very likely to lose a large percentage of their population because of extreme hunger. Efforts to provide relief have failed, and reports of mismanagement abound.

According to an article in <u>National Geographic,</u> in the USA, record numbers of people are without enough food (August 2021, p86-109). Food insecurity has become a fact of life for many. The locations include large cities and rural areas where COVID has hit hard, mainly where interactions with drought, famine, and flooding have occurred.

Primary Effect

The primary effect is that many people, especially children, lose their lives, as do the elderly and handicapped. Many lose their livelihoods and must re-locate. In many cases, this requires selling land at low prices and hoping that employment can be achieved in a new locale.

It also requires that other crop areas can make up for the lost farmland. If not, prices are bound to arise, and they may increase anyway as cropland is gradually lost across the country. In time, this leads to villages and towns collapsing and drying up.

Animals must be sold or slaughtered. This causes fluctuations in the cost of meats and other goods, thereby causing additional hardships for folks.

Spin-off Effects

The spin-off effects are, to a large extent, continuations of the Primary Effects. Over time, either the land again becomes able to support life, or it turns into a desolate, if not hostile, environment.

Earthquakes

Primary Effects

Earthquakes are classified according to:

- Cause of origin (tectonic or non-tectonic).
- Depth of hypocenter: The depth at which the earthquake originates determines the strength of the earthquake. Surface earthquakes less than 10 km deep are very intense. (Jayeshe, 2012)
- Intensity and magnitude: Intensity is the degree of damage and destruction caused by the earthquake.

The closer to the epicenter, the more damage the area will encounter. Magnitude measures the energy of the earthquake. ("Have Earthquakes Increased?"(2014).

Earthquake frequencies of magnitude 5.5 Mw have increased in the past nine years. In Mexico, in September 2021, an earthquake occurred with terrible outcomes. There were many dead, homes and other structures were destroyed, and flooding covered large swaths of land.

Many individuals are unaware of the number of earthquakes that take place around them. For example, the North Carolina Department of Public Safety reports that since 1735 North Carolina has experienced 23 damaging earthquakes. Many more of a lesser strength have been recorded.

The "Great Shake Out" is an international movement to increase awareness by promoting annual drills on International Shake Out Day. The website shakeout.org offers information about earthquake safety and how to plan and host their own earthquake drills.

However, professors of the National Academy of Science have stated that earthquakes over 8 Mw are no more than past earthquake cycles. The increase in more minor earthquakes is the after-shocks of the significant earthquakes in 2004 in Sumatra and 2011 in Northeastern Japan ("Have Earthquakes Increased?", 2008). No need to panic yet!

However, there are long-term effects of some earthquakes. The March 11, 2011, earthquake in Japan generated a tsunami with a maximum wave height of almost 40 meters (130 feet) in the Iwate Prefecture. Researchers also determined that the tsunami impacted a 2,000-kilometer (1,242-mile) stretch of Japan's Pacific coast.

A tsunami disabled the power supply and cooling of three Fukushima Daiichi nuclear reactors following the earthquake, causing a significant nuclear accident. All three nuclear cores melted mainly in the first three days, and thirty years later, the nearby lake was still radioactive. This consequence is a precise instance of cascading with horrendous results and long-term outcomes.

The 2011 Fukushima nuclear disaster will cost hundreds of billions of dollars to clean. Still, a study claims the environmental cost could be significantly higher, with nearby lakes contaminated for another 20 years.

A group of researchers, led by those at the University of Tsukuba, have found that Lake Onuma on Mount Akagi could be contaminated with radioactive cesium-137 (137CS) for roughly 30 years after the disaster.

As of December 2020, the Japan National Police Agency reported 15,899 deaths, 2,527 missing and presumed deaths, and 6,157 injuries for the Great East Japan event.

However, there is a concern for the future as global warming continues and glaciers melt, causing water weight to shift on the earth's crust. These actions may also cause earthquakes ("Have Earthquakes Increased?" 2008).

Earthquakes can cause minor damage and no loss of life, and they can also destroy all physical structures in their path and cause immense loss of life and injuries. One of its most profound effects is that they can occur with no warning, often at night.

The USA has been fortunate for the most part to have escaped a high frequency of severe quakes, excluding Alaska. However, that is not likely to last forever.

Many, if not most Americans, do not realize that the most dangerous fault line, known as the Cascadia subduction zone, runs for 700 miles off the coast of the Pacific Northwest, beginning near Cape Mendocino, California, and terminating around Vancouver Island, Canada. The quake from this fault, according to Kenneth Murphy, Director of FEMA"s Region X (Oregon, Washington, Idaho, and Alaska) (March, 2018) and says such a quake will mean "everything west of Interstate 5 will be toast." This seems to be a matter of "when," not "if."

Spin-Off Effects

Three significant spin-off effects are loss of power, loss of transportation systems, and loss food and essential goods delivery systems. Loss of drinking water and damaged sewer systems can quickly lead to infectious diseases.

One very dangerous spin-off occurs when the earthquake is in the ocean or a significant impact event. It can cause a severe displacement of vast amounts of water which can reach astounding heights. The Tsunami resulting from the impact in the Gulf of Mexico, which contributed to the demise of the dinosaurs, has been estimated as a mile high.

The average Tsunami is not a mile high, but it can be highly damaging. The consequences can be many deaths and injured. They roar ashore, pushing everything in their path ahead of it and destroying most physical structures they encounter. It is not unusual for the tsunami wave to reach one mile inland.

A spin-off effect of the impact event is the potential for large amounts of dust and dirt to be thrown in large quantities into the sky. This could result in winds that block out the sun for long periods.

Floods

Floods occur from several causes, depending mainly on their type. There are generally considered to be either four or five types of flooding, and the five types are:

- Areal Floods. This type of flood is prevalent in flatter areas where the water table is shallow.
- Catastrophic Floods. As the name implies, a sudden change in the environment or infrastructure results in significant flooding.
- Coastal (Estuarine) Floods. Caused mainly by low barometric -pressure or high winds from one direction or channel floods from the other, coastal floods can result from tropical storms, cyclones, or even secondary flooding following a tsunami.

In cases of flooding inland, the floods are often created by massive waves.

- Riverine Floods. All have in common that stream and river channels can take on a sudden influx of water far more enormous than they can contain. The water level rises quickly and usually turns muddy due to the amount of sediment being washed away. Dry areas with deep but narrow rivers are prone to flooding, but even wetter climates aren't immune.

Riverine floods pose several dangers. Not only can flash floods rapidly overtake low-lying roads and residential areas, but the sudden rush of water is enough to rip open land, trees, and anything else along the riverbanks. Due to the speed of the water, it's easy for people to get swept up and drown. The force of the water is often strong enough to force homes from their foundations and turn cars into upside-down boats.

- Urban Flooding. Caused by flash floods, excessive rain, or broken water mains, urban floods are any form of inundation occurring in densely populated areas. Areas with poor drainage and sewage systems are more prone to this sort of flooding.

Because flood waters have a habit of seeping into basements or coming into contact with sewage, areas suffering from urban flooding may be required to use bottled water or even evacuate until the flood recedes and cleanup may begin.

Primary Effects

Depending on which type of flood is involved, deaths may be a significant effect. Even shallow water can result in drowning. Surface water is a particularly critical situation for children who can be swept up or lose their footing in shallow water and not be able to regain their footing.

The types of flooding that produce the most threat of deaths are catastrophic, coastal, and riverine, but all are dangerous.

Particularly of note is flooding in home basements, apartments below ground level, and buildings whose structure may be corroded by salt water.

Spin-Off Effects

Due to the speed with which flooding can occur, many people are caught without adequate preparation.

Streams and rivers overflowing their banks create hazardous conditions. This can happen in an amazingly short time trapping many folks in their attics or on their roofs. Not many folks store boats in their attics or on roofs, so they are left without transportation. They are essentially trapped until a rescue boat reaches them or the water recedes.

One of the spin-off effects is the need to be adequately prepared. To do so will cost money in advance, but if a flood occurred, it would be money well spent. Evacuation and emergency packs need to be prepared and available at a moment's notice. Drinking water may become contaminated, and a supply of fresh water, enough for several days' use, should be available.

Obtaining food could become a problem. A small

camp stove should be available for cooking. Power may be unavailable for days or weeks, if not longer.

In southern states, snakes and alligators pose a real risk.

Depending on the weather, a generator may prove a precious asset for heat, charging phones, etc. Fuel for it must be available for several days.

Hurricanes

Primary Effects

Hurricanes are a significant concern for the Eastern Sea Board and the Southern coast. It is unlikely that inhabitants of Kansas need to spend much time being concerned about hurricanes. However, they may need to be concerned with some of the spin-off effects.

Hurricanes (also called tropical cyclones in places) have a history of being erratic and very dangerous and costly. The data support these beliefs and also provide the basis for examining the primary and spin-off effects.

There are three significant primary effects; each by itself can cause untold deaths and damage. These are the winds, the storm surge, and the flooding. Taken together, they have caused some of the highest death tolls, the most extensive damage, the longest-lasting damage and recovery period, and the most expensive to repair of any of the types of national disasters.

Cumulatively, hurricanes have caused the most damage, caused the most deaths, ruined the most physical structures, and cost any number of billions of dollars for recovery efforts. Hurricanes are fueled by warm water and climate change heating. As these variables increase, the damages they will cause can be expected to increase proportionally.

Spin-Off Effects

The spin-off effects can be worse than the actual storm and last much longer. Storm surges can sweep far inland, causing floods, loss of power, and stranding many folks in their homes, attics, or roofs.

Further, inland streams may overflow, farm animals may be lost, and safe drinking water may not exist.

The loss of power in cities may mean loss of sewage systems, and safe drinking water may not be available. It would have to be trucked in if roadways are passable.

Schools may be closed, possibly serving as shelters. Shops and stores may be closed, leading to a shortage of food.

Many Americans think hurricanes are a southern problem only. Not so! Many hurricanes have made their way northward, causing massive flooding across the mid-east and into New England with heavy loss of life.

Land Slides (Includes Mud Slides)

Landslides are not as numerous as many other types of disasters. Nevertheless, they can be devastating when they occur in occupied areas. They are included under Level 1 disasters because of the finality they bring to the site they submerge.

Primary Effects

The primary effect of a Landslide is that everything in its path can be buried under tons of rocks, dirt and whatever physical structures were in its way. These include trees, homes, sheds, power grids, etc. And, of course, the bodies of all those caught in its path. In many cases, the size of boulders and the depth of the slide prohibit the rapid recovery of those lost.

The slide is often precipitated by massive rain storms over a short time. The slide usually begins on mountain crests or tops in mountainous areas where there tend to be small villages. There is often no warning except for a growing roar signifying its arrival.

Spin-Off Effects

The spin-off effects are generally determined by whether the slide is in an inhabited area. If it is, then the principal side effect is the damage done to life and village wellbeing.

Many times, the village is inaccessible due to damage done to roads and infrastructure. Food and water can also be very difficult commodities to find. Medical assistance may not be available. Helicopters may be the only means of contact. Electrical grids and telephones may not be working.

At times the slide may miss villages but cover roads, even interstate highways, to the extent that passage is impossible. This causes delays, sometimes extensive ones, in necessary resources reaching remote villages or communities. Ham radio operators can be life savers at such times.

Thunder Storms

Thunderstorms and their associated lightning strikes are probably the most familiar of any disaster type. Perhaps, for this reason, they are often dismissed as not thing more than a nuisance, and this is a big mistake.

Primary Effects

Thunder, by itself, is not dangerous. Noisy, and at times scary, but not dangerous.

The worst primary effect of a thunderstorm is a lightning strike. A strike can have one of four effects. One, it hits nothing, and so it has a net impact of zero. Second, it can hit a person or group of people, causing deaths and severe burns. Third, it can hit a physical structure, causing it to burst into flame or explode. Fourth, it can hit a wooded or forested area and begin a wildfire.

Spin-Off Effects

The spin-off effects of numbers two, three, or four can have shattering effects on families, homes, and communities. At times all three can be shattered by one lightning strike.

A wildfire can cause untold damage to crops, loss of forest land, loss of wildlife, and entire communities before it can be brought under control (more in the section on wildfires).

Lighting can also cause severe problems with the electric grid and all that it controls.

Unfortunately, a considerable amount of data suggests many wildfires are set either deliberately or by human accident.

Tornadoes

Tornadoes are among the most feared of all-natural disasters. They are unstoppable, and the destruction they wreak is hard to believe.

Primary Effects

Anything in the path of a tornado is in for a hard time. All can be destroyed from humans and animals to cars, homes, barns, bridges, and wide swaths of communities, towns, and cities. It goes without saying that power grids will be torn apart, as will water and sewage systems.

Spin-Off Effects

It is hard to imagine the despair that many folks have after coming back to find their home destroyed. In such a case, all their belongings are likely to be strewn over a two-county area. Depression is not an uncommon result in such a situation. Financial ruin is a real possibility.

It is even worse if a portion of the community, including schools, stores, banks, and other essential services ceases to exist. The thought of having to re-build all can be crushing. The emotional and financial toll can drive many to despair.

Tropical Cyclone (Essentially the same as Hurricanes)

Solar Flares

Solar flares rarely intrude on most people's thoughts, and they are seldom discussed in mainstream news and even more rarely seen without the aid of special equipment.

At a 2021 conference data communication conference held by SIGCOMM and reported by Brandon Specktor in MSN News, the results of extreme space weather could be catastrophic to our modern way of life. Specktor says a severe solar storm could turn into an "internet Apocalypse" with the internet offline for weeks or months.

Primary Effects

The effect of solar flares is on the earth's electrical grid but even more so on its communications systems that depend on the network of satellites that ring the planet. Many believe it is only a matter of time till a solar flare occurs that is strong enough to cancel the satellites and most of the earth's electrical grids.

The problem is that extreme solar storms (also called coronal mass ejections) are relatively rare. According to a conference paper, scientists estimate the probability of extreme space weather directly impacting Earth to be between 1.6% to 12% per decade.

Only two such storms have been recorded in recent history — one in 1859 and the other in 1921. The earlier incident, known as the Carrington Event, created such a severe geomagnetic disturbance on Earth that telegraph wires burst into flame. Auroras — usually only visible near the planet's poles — were spotted near-equatorial Colombia. Smaller storms can also pack a punch; one in March 1989 blacked out the entire Canadian province of Quebec for nine hours.

Since then, Loving Systems has become much more reliant on the global internet. According to Abdu Jyothi, the potential impacts of a massive geomagnetic storm on that new infrastructure remain largely unstudied. In her latest paper on this topic, she tried to pinpoint the most significant vulnerabilities in that infrastructure.

The good news is, that local and regional internet connections are likely at low risk of being damaged. Fiber-optic cables themselves aren't affected by geomagnetically induced currents, according to Jyothi's paper.

However, the long undersea internet cables that connect continents are a different story. These cables are equipped with repeaters to boost the optical signal, spaced at intervals of roughly 30 to 90 miles (50 to 150 kilometers). These repeaters are vulnerable to geomagnetic currents. Entire cables could be made useless if even one repeater goes offline, according to the paper.

Abdu Jyothi wrote that if enough undersea cables fail in a particular region, entire continents could be cut off from one another. Furthermore, nations at high latitudes — such as the U.S. and the U.K. — are far more susceptible to solar weather than nations at lower latitudes. In the event of a catastrophic geomagnetic storm, it's those high-latitude nations that are most likely to be cut off from the network first. It's hard to predict how long it would take to repair underwater infrastructure, but Abdu Jyothi suggests large-scale internet outages that last weeks or months are possible.

In the meantime, millions of people could lose their livelihoods. "The economic impact of an Internet disruption for a day in the US is estimated to be over $7 billion," Abdu Jyothi wrote in her paper. "What if the network remains non-functional for days or even months?"

Suppose we don't want to find out. In that case, grid operators need to start taking the threat of extreme solar weather seriously, as global internet infrastructure inevitably expands. Laying more cables at lower latitudes is a good start, Abdu Jyothi said, as is developing resilience tests that focus on the effects of large-scale network failures.

When the next big solar storm does blast out of our star, people on Earth will have about 13 hours to prepare for its arrival, she added. Let's hope we're ready to make the most of that time when it inevitably arrives.

Spin-Off Effects

If such an effect occurred, it would send the earth back to a time of smoke signals and drawing water from wells. Without power, industries could not operate, hospitals would have to curtail their services severely, and horses and buggies would again be the norm.

Virus

As we have all learned during the past couple of years, a virus can turn into an international pandemic in an astonishingly short period.

Primary Effects

From the beginning, it has to be realized that politics and narcissism played a severe disrupting role in promoting best practices for dealing with COVID-19. It is impressive, even still, that effective vaccines were developed as quickly as they were.

It was not just in the USA where effective leadership was lacking. In dealing with just one aspect of Climate Change, 'global warming' U.N. Secretary-General Antonio Guterres said at the beginning of the 2021 climate summit in Glasgow, Scotland, "the current emissions gap is the result of a leadership gap." And keep in mind, this was referring to only one segment of a much larger problem. That is encompassing the entirety of a climate change inter-related set of planet-wide problems.

There were two areas of primary effect. The first was the

physical and cognitive effect on individuals who contracted the virus and those who cared for them. Many succumbed to the virus. The hospital staff was tragically shorthanded, and ICU rooms were hard to find.

Families of the ill were unsure where to turn for answers and assistance. When the political leaders ignore the problem, say it is inaccurate, and refuse to accept the data of world-trusted research agencies, where does the individual family turn? The cumulative effect was to add another layer of stress on those who were already nearly stressed out.

The second effect was on the psyche of those who treated the ill. This group included the concerned families, those who lost their jobs and livelihood due to the virus, and its secondary effects.

It is hypothesized that the effect on this group was for many the driver that generated many of the social disorders that were evidenced.

For many, the loss of a job without an alternative means of income meant a loss of control of their life. Unable to assess the situation more realistically, thousands denied they were responsible for their loss and projected blame on too many others. Others caused the problem, so the individuals felt justified in taking their frustration and anger out on them. All too often, these individuals felt superior to many on some basis or were faceless individuals who just happened to be in the wrong place at the wrong time.

Spin-Off Effects

The spin-off effects were as confusing as could be without purposely trying to confuse things. Masks were to be worn but not in all places. Education was the most seriously disrupted, with many school systems and universities resorting to remote learning. The data has since indicated that many students had difficulty learning apace with classroom learning and suffered measurable losses. The very important role that structured education plays in socialization was neglected entirely. Many parents lost income because their time had to be with their children during the day.

It has to be concluded that schools' responses to the situation were dismal, particularly in two general areas. First, students learn better in a social situation. Education decision-makers either forgot this or did not have the insight to think of other ways of grouping students. Second, at the adolescent level, who monitored the students at home to ensure they spent their time on schoolwork? Without daily supervision, many adolescents roamed the streets day and night. With guns being as easy to obtain as they are, many adolescents used them for drive-by shootings, robberies, gang warfare, and murder.

Businesses resorted to working from home and whether this was an advantage and to whom is not known.

Many small businesses and restaurants had to close, with many unable to open again. The financial and emotional stress placed on many was substantial and significant.

Volcano Eruptions

Fortunately, volcano eruptions are not very numerous during any given year. However, when they do erupt, they are devastating to everything in their path.

Primary Effects

The primary Effects of volcanos are well known. And, they generally give signals that they are about to erupt. Being not very numerous is very fortunate for those who heed the signs, not so much for those who ignore them. These include the signals that animals, dogs mainly, emit before an eruption.

The primary effect of a volcanic eruption is that everything in its path is burnt or buried beneath feet of volcanic ash. This ash can be from a few inches to many feet deep. And it can turn into a hardened mass; Pompeii provides more than ample evidence of how deep, and complex this mass can become over time.

Spin-Off Effects

Side effects depend on the amount of build-up of ash and lava around the volcano. When there have been previous eruptions, the buildup should be slight. If, however, there have been years or decades between eruptions, there may be considerable buildup with people believing the volcano will not erupt again, or at least in their lifetime.

If the volcano does erupt, and depending on how large an eruption it is and the path chosen by the lava, more or less of whatever is in its course will be destroyed.

Wildfires

Heat waves have engulfed large sections of the American North West, down through California, into Nevada, Arizona, and Texas, creating wildfires beyond belief. The damages have been beyond extensive. Thousands of homes and other physical structures have been destroyed.

It is just not in America that these fires have created havoc. Germany, Spain, Canada, Bolivia, Brazil, and England have all experienced wildfires unheard of at a level not seen before. Russia has in Siberia a fire that is greater than all of the rest of the countries combined.

Primary Effects

The most significant loss has been the loss of life and the thousands of structures, including hundreds of homes. Countess acres of forest have been consumed. Entire communities have been leveled. For many, no end is in sight. French farmers had to watch their animals burn,

The driver for the fires has been constant heat waves, in many states reaching record highs. And behind these heat waves is the rising temperature of the oceans as a result of climate change.

Public health experts already know communities of color are often more likely to experience childhood asthma and live in places that exacerbate it. That risk increases in African-American people from 34% to 41%, as the climate warms, according to the report, which analyzed projected risks.

African American people are also 40% more likely to live in areas with deaths related to extreme weather temperatures. As the temperature of the planet increases, that risk rises to 59%.

The report also highlights certain risks to Hispanic and Latino people, overrepresented in construction and agriculture jobs. As the climate warms, they are 43% more likely to live in areas with hours on the job cut due to extreme temperatures.

In larger cities, one can trace where more well-to-do

citizens live by the number and size of trees in their neighborhood; they are plentiful. As the income level goes down, so does the number of trees in the district until practically none exist. The presence or absence of trees can mean a difference of nearly two degrees. (Borunda, 2021, <u>National Geographic</u>.)

It does not seem possible that many still deride the notion of climate change. These nay-sayers are probably the same individuals who claim there is no need for vaccines or masks to help deal with COVID-19. They scorn the notion of science, although the sciences have provided the conveniences they enjoy today.

The wildfires running through these countries and states have rendered power lines non-existent, exacerbated the drought conditions in many areas, caused cattlemen to auction off many of their cattle, and caused farmers to lose crops for several years. Entire towns have been razed, including all the homes and businesses contained within.

Spin-Off Effects

The spin-off effects have been nearly as harmful as the primary effects.

Perhaps the most dangerous spin-off effect is the respiratory deaths caused by burning. This effect has spanned oceans to generate an estimated one million deaths in the past year (Gardiner, Beth, April 2021, National Geographic, 41-78).

These effects have worsened existing droughts and caused water shortages in many areas over large portions of land. Lakes in California are at historic lows. The water from the Colorado River will be cut for the first time in history.

The giant aquifer underlying much of America's South West is rapidly being depleted due to prolonged use and drought conditions. It will take decades of rain and no use before it replenishes itself.

LEVEL 2 DISASTERS

Level 2 Disasters are placed in this category not because they are less dangerous than those in Level 1. However, they tend to be less frequent, less intense, or not as widespread as Level 1 disasters.

Avalanche

Many of the same comments made concerning landslides also pertain to avalanches. Obviously, though, avalanches occur with snow and ice. This can complicate and extend the recovery progress to a significant degree. Also, with the reduction of ice and snow in many areas, there may be a reduction in avalanches.

Many avalanches occur in remote areas where rescue crews and resources are in short supply. Just finding any individuals caught in an avalanche can consume vast amounts of time. Helicopters can help a great deal but need a focal point to begin looking for lost skiers, among others.

Remote communities can be cut off for days, or longer, and food supplies can have difficulty getting to the towns. Obviously, towns need to be prepared by stockpiling necessary goods. Medical and evacuation services can be accomplished via helicopters.

Blizzards/Cold Waves

Blizzards and natural cold waves are not much of a concern to those who live in Louisiana. However, they can be a dangerous hazard to those who live in states where they do occur.

Thanks to weather forecasters, folks are usually warned ahead of time of blizzards and cold waves. And those who live in blizzard-prone zones should be stocked up on necessary commodities.

Hail/Ice Storms

Hail and ice storms are not generally considered to be major natural disasters. However, if you are a farmer and your crop should be destroyed by a hail storm, you would think it to be a natural disaster

Likewise, if you are caught in an ice storm while running out of gas, you could be in a difficult situation, especially if you don't have a phone. If you have sufficient gas, your best play is to wait for melting.

LEVEL 3 DISASTERS

Impact Event

An impact event can range from no effect to a catastrophic outcome depending on two major factors. These are one, whether the impact is on land or water, and, two, the size of the impact.

Primary Effects

The primary effect is if the meteor is a decent size (for example, at least 10 meters in diameter). If the impact is on land in a desolate area, a massive hole in the ground and the loss of any trees can be expected. If the impact is in a medium-size city the loss of the city can be expected, as can the loss of surrounding suburbs with a high percentage of deaths.

If the impact is in water and far from shore, a tsunami can be expected to reach the coast but at an indeterminate height. However, if the impact is closer to shore, a tsunami of significant proportions can be expected. There would also be large amounts of dirt and such, possibly, but probably not leading to a nuclear winter.

The situation evolving from the damage to the three nuclear reactors in Japan in DATE? as the result of an underwater earthquake and the resulting tsunami are evidence of the number of lives lost and the tremendous amount of damage and costs that can result in even 30 years after the event.

Cascading Disasters

Unfortunately, there are many incidents of natural disasters occurring in quick succession or overlapping in time. This type of event series causes immense damage to the physical structures as well as the social fabric.

Haiti is a case in point. During the spring and summer of 2021, it was already reeling from the effects of the pandemic. Its medical services structure was severely weakened from tending to the ill. Its financial services were weak from years of abuse. In effect, it was an emerging country struggling to stay afloat.

Then on August 14, 2021, a hurricane, closely followed by a 7.2 earthquake, (usgs.gov) swept through, followed closely by 900 after quakes and significant flooding that added to the devastation caused by the previous flooding. Overall, COVID hung like a dark cloud. (Wallace, Wu and Patal, 2021).

The Washington Post and the New York Times have each been reporting on conditions in Haiti. (Opinion

Drug trafficking and an assassination have deepened Haiti's chaos, Editorial Board, Washington Post, December 14, 2021). Social disorder and gangs running amok have frequently been reported. The cascade of natural disasters only deepened what was a country floundering amid a host of overwhelming problems.

Haiti had been a developing country. Its law enforcement services were unable to keep pace with the growing social chaos and gang-related activities.

It is clear that the convergence of disasters in a small, developing country, located in a dangerous location for natural disasters to strike, led to a mixture of natural disasters and social disorder. Only by understanding the interrelationships among the various parts will some understanding of the processes by which they work to be achieved.

Electric Grid Failures

Electrical grid failures are placed here because they can fail from several Part A disasters, as well as several from Part B. Spin-off effects from several disasters can cause failures on a local, state, or regional level. In an extreme situation, a country-wide failure could occur. Obviously, they can also fail from cyber-attacks. More is said about these failures under the appropriate descriptions of each disaster.

In addition to the specific type of disasters that have devastated large portions of the country, they have appeared in an increasing cascade of over-lapping catastrophes. Wildfires in California, and the entire Northwest, accompanied by flooding and lake levels dropping to unheard-of levels; droughts in the Southwest with floods and impoverished aquifers being drained so low that decades, if not centuries, will be needed to restore their levels to those of just a few years ago. Other examples are easily found, for example, the increased ferocity and damage caused by hurricanes and coastal storms.

The physical, economic, and emotional drain on people in these affected areas has been significant. And, then the COVID, with its several variants, which at this writing do not seem to have diminished, settled over the country like an oppressive blanket, adding its misery to that already being suffered by the populace.

It is the combination of the cascading effect of the disasters that delivered crippling blows to the physical, financial, social, and personal elements of the country. The COVID was bad enough but putting political agendas above the needs of the populace only exacerbated the difficulties of trying to cope effectively with all of the disasters' influences.

PART A

CLIMATE CHANGE

TEMPERATURE RISE LEADS TO

WARMER WATER

LEADS TO

ICE MELTING   HURRICANES   HEAT WAVES

FLOODING STORM SURGES WILD FIRES

DROUGHTS FAMINES HUNGER

THUNDER STORMS, TORNADOS ELEC GRID FAILS

EARTHQUAKES/TUSMANIS

AND TO

SOCIAL DISORDERS

PART B

NON-CLIMATE CHANGE

HAIL STORMS

COLD WAVES

AVALANCE

FOG

BLIZZARDS

IMPACT EVENT

LINEMIC ERUPTION

CHAPTER 6

SOCIAL DISORDERS AND THE ROLE OF NATURAL DISASTERS

There is any number of factors that affect an individual's sense of well-being. These include age, gender, race, economic status, physical condition, social anxiety, susceptibility to depression, and others. Stress is often a daily companion that varies up and down with changes in daily activities, environmental intrusions, as well as personal history, and interactions.

There is any number of situations that an individual may experience that cause succumbing to feelings of alienation in a non-disaster environment. However, being in such an environment increases the chances, particularly for those who tend to operate on the fringes of society, are an outlier, are psychologically weakened, or are in a low economic situation. There seems little doubt that the overall stress level increased among workers during 2021.

Gallup's "State of the Global Workplace: 2021 Report" found that workers in the US and Canada reported the highest levels of daily stress in the world last year, with 57% percent of US and Canadian workers experiencing high day-to-day pressure. Between the two countries, Canadian workers reported more significant daily stress and worry than their US counterparts.

Globally, a record 43% of workers reported an increase in daily stress last year, up from 38% feeling in 2019, raising concerns about burnout after a particularly difficult year at work.

US and Canadian workers were also the most stressed in the world in pre-pandemic 2019, according to Gallup.

There are antecedents and consequences, as well as interrelationships among these variables of burnout, stress, and other factors. Together, they represent a considerable obstacle to daily living. Under COVID conditions, they raised stress levels to extreme heights. And to the difficulties posed by these conditions, another was added.

In its August 2021 issue, <u>National Geographic</u> devoted an entire section to "America's Hunger Crisis." After some gains following the recession of 2007-09, up to 2019, the pandemic shut these gains down. The most brutally hit of all were communities of color, where food-in security was common among non-white households.

This is one of the major problems encountered in natural disasters. One condition may cascade into others, multiplying the original problem many times over. It is a case where a non-linear perspective can provide a helpful process for identifying the probable types of cascading disasters and the probable outcomes, including second-level effects.

The following table depicts how increasing stress caused by natural disasters may lead to personal and social disorders.

These lists are not meant to be all-inclusive. There are probably many more underlying factors that could and do lead to these behaviors. All of them do occur without the stress of a pandemic. However, each of them has increased in frequency since the pandemic's start time

Emma Tucker and Peter Nickeas of CNN reported on April 3, 2021, 63 of the 66 largest police jurisdictions saw increases in at least one category of violent crimes in 2020. These include homicide, rape, robbery, and aggravated assault, according to a report produced by the Major Cities Chiefs Association.

Covid-19 seemed to exacerbate everything -- officers sometimes had to quarantine because of exposure or cases in their ranks, reducing the number of officers available for patrol, investigations, or protest coverage. It was difficult to impossible to keep physical distance during protests.

Through the first three months of 2021, many major cities have indicated they are still experiencing high rates of violent crime, according to Laura Cooper, executive director of the Major Cities Chiefs Association.

On April 8, 2020 Covid-19 seemed to exacerbate everything -- officers sometimes had to quarantine because of exposure or cases in their ranks, reducing the number of officers available for patrol, investigations, or protest coverage. It was difficult to impossible to keep physical distance during protests.

Through the first three months of 2021, many major cities indicated they were still experiencing high rates of violent crime, according to Laura Cooper, executive director of the Major Cities Chiefs Association.

Ashley Abramson, reporting for the American

Psychological Association, on April 8, 2021, wrote about how COVID-19 may increase domestic violence and child abuse.

As the nation grappled with the spread of COVID-19, Americans were being told to go home and stay there, for their safety and everyone else's. However, for victims and survivors of domestic violence, including children exposed to it, being home may not be a safe option — and the unprecedented stress of the pandemic could breed fear, anger, and violence in homes where violence may not have been an issue before.

According to the National Coalition Against Domestic Violence, from 2016 through 2018 the number of intimate partner violence victimizations in the United States increased by 42%.

- On a typical day, domestic violence hotlines nationwide receive over 19,000 calls.
- An abuser's access to a firearm increases the risk of intimate partner femicide by 400%.
- In 2018, partner violence accounted for 20% of all violent crimes.
- Intimate partner violence is most common against women between the ages of 18-24.
- 19% of intimate partner violence involves a weapon.

Impact

Domestic violence is prevalent in every community and affects all people regardless of age, socioeconomic status, sexual orientation, gender, race, religion, or nationality.

Physical violence is often accompanied by emotionally abusive and controlling behavior as part of a much larger, systematic pattern of dominance and control. Domestic violence can result in physical injury, psychological trauma, and even death. The devastating consequences of domestic violence can cross generations and last a lifetime

According to the Centers for Disease Control and Prevention, 1 in 3 women and 1 in 4 men in the United States have experienced violence from an intimate partner in their lifetime— and the risks to victims are severe. CDC data link intimate partner violence with an increased risk of injury and death. About 41% of female intimate partner violence survivors and 14% of male intimate partner violence survivors sustain a physical injury from their abusers. About 1 in 6 homicide victims are killed by their private partners.

It is entirely possible that the loss of a job with no immediate prospect of another one can be interpreted as a loss of control over important aspects of one's life, as well as a loss of position and power within the home. These losses may breed the need to regain some ego or control by exercising dominance over a spouse or child. Likewise, these feelings of lack of control may lead to violence executed toward those perceived as inferior or to blame for the individual's loss.

Violence in the home can also lead to adverse health and mental health outcomes, including a higher risk of chronic disease, depression, post-traumatic stress disorder, and risky sexual and substance use behaviors.

Now, experts worry that all these numbers could increase dramatically during this period of social distancing and quarantine. Psychologist Josie Serrata, Ph.D., a research and evaluation consultant, has found in her research that stress and social isolation can raise the risk of domestic violence. (Serrata, Josie, 2021, https://www.vitadox.com)

It can also escalate outside the home. The number of increases in mass shootings, the number of senseless drive-by shootings, the rise in the number of weapons brought to school, the increase in the number of random assaults, and the rise in the number and severe types of assaults on airline personnel all speak to the impulsive nature of the behavior. Such behaviors don't occur after re-mediated careful thought. They erupt out of reaching a frustration level beyond the individual's ability or desire to control. It is not insignificant that the number of assaults on people of color, including Asians, the homeless, or unarmed women, has significantly increased. (Serrata, Josie, 2021, https://www.vitadox.com).

In her 2019 study on how Hurricane Harvey affected families that had already experienced domestic violence, Serrata found the stress associated with the disaster led to higher rates of both domestic violence and child abuse during and after the hurricane.

There seems little doubt that natural disasters, particularly if they cascade, are national in effect or last for a prolonged time, leading to various social disorders of an increasingly intensive and violent nature. What may start by being on a drinking binge leads to increased acting out behavior against others of a different color, gender, or language. This may escalate into gang behavior with little or no focus on a particular type of person. In turn, this may escalate into a more expansive city or region-wide rebellion.

Nazi Germany is an example of the possibility of expansion to a country-wide disorder.

A Future Emergence

There is a newly emerging aspect to social disorders that cannot be totally attributed to natural disasters. This is concerned with the possibility that the violence evidenced in so many social disorders of late is a consequence of the social distancing seen during the COVID years, combined with the behaviors developed during those trying times. The cumulative effect of constant and repetitive disasters combined with the nationwide suffocating effect of COVID laid a pall of despair over the country. This was accompanied by an ever-increasing rise in the level of stress experienced by many.

With so many of the recent violent events attributed to adolescents, there is a good chance that the remote learning enforced by so many schools did not provide the social structure and learning environments needed by students for their development. This was exacerbated by more parents having to be out of the home working and the lack of community programs that could provide needed support. The ease with which 18-year-olds could purchase guns is so stupid it is not worth remarking about.

The violence demonstrated lately is a consequence of these factors plus children not being taught impulse control behaviors by parents or how and why to empathize with the plights of others. This is not to suggest these behaviors are typical of most parents. With more parents out of the home longer, the lack of funds, and loss of jobs put enormous stress on family dynamics during the COVID years. It was unfortunate political leaders did not have the understanding necessary to provide a coordinated plan of assistance and support.

There is also the possibility that so many students from a young age have played video games that include killing on a large scale. They come to believe such is common. Then they all come back alive at the end of the game. It is not real, but in the absence of a monitor for these games, much reality is lost and carried over into real life.

The danger of these behaviors continuing to be exhibited during the coming years is high due to two factors. The first is that there will be the typical demands to punish those responsible for these violent behaviors. This is understandable but does not help in understanding how to identify early those with the greatest likelihood of displaying these behaviors so that helpful preventive solutions can be developed and implemented

This is important for two reasons. The first is to aid those currently afflicted by these impulses.

The second is a longer-range concern, and perhaps more critical. It is highly probable that within the next 20 years the nation and planet will be plagued with storms, droughts, famines, lack of potable water, rising sea levels, shortages of necessities, and other disasters that will act to compress living areas into smaller and smaller areas. This will increase stress to levels currently unimaginable.

In the United States Lauren Leffer, writing in Gizmodo describes the ongoing drought as becoming increasingly desperate.

It is well within the realm of possibility that as some

counties are deprived of the basic needs of life that they will begin taking from their neighbors, resulting in growing wars to obtain what they need. The Catholic Agency for Overseas Development, in a report by Ngala Chimtom, reports that famine in the Horn of Africa will affect 20 million people. The levels of violence will escalate unless imaginative thinking is allowed to develop preventive and supportive programs before the worst of the climate changes take place.

Man-made disasters must also be entered into the equation. Currently, we are approaching a planet-wide famine, fed in large part by the Russian-Ukraine war. This war is blocking the delivery of huge amounts of grain, much of being destined for Africa. As famines increase amidst increasing drought conditions, rising sea waters, and compressed land for living, it is to be expected that local, regional, and national battles will erupt.

There are cities today that are attempting to address the rising seas with makeshift remedies. The homes being swept away in North Carolina by rising sea levels are a harbinger of things to come. These rising sea levels are made worse by a sinking Atlantic Sea Bed. NOAA reports that an Ecological disaster is about to hit the North Carolina coast.

California reported an increase in highway shootings that doubled from 210 in 2019 to nearly 500 in the first 11 months of 2021.

No one city will be able to allocate the resources necessary to address the problem. It will take a regional plan at the very least to deal adequately with the coming problems, and a national or planet-wide approach would be preferable.

During the past few years, the sounds of alarm have been increasing. But with the demands on their attention generated by the COVID problems legislatures have not given adequate thought to the long-term needs brought on by climate change. It is not likely that this will change. Given the political climate in Washington and the perceived need to raise ever more funding for re-election campaigns, it does not appear hopeful that legislators will devote much thought or commitment to developing long-term programs to deal with the coming storm. A new approach is necessary to cope with the scope of the problems.

The urgency with which these problems must be addressed is seen by looking at a world map. Natural and human developed disasters in South America, famine and droughts in Africa, the usual boiling pots of discord in the middle east, the increasing nuclear and unpredictable Iran, and the expansionist plans of Russia and China cannot be addressed with solely a linear approach. A non-linear concept and plan which seeks to establish and understand the system interactions among these various areas are needed.

CHAPTER 7

A PROPOSAL FOR CHANGE

Unfortunately, it is abundantly clear that the political leadership around the world (see results of COP26) is totally incapable of responding to the urgency of the climate crisis in anything other than verbal promises for something half a century hence. There are a number of possible reasons for this lack of action, any or all of which could explain their lack of effort.

1. They don't comprehend the dire and growing urgency of addressing the crisis with other than meaningless words.
2. Their inability to act on issues beyond tomorrow's problems or re-election fund drives.
3. The inability to think and act as one body to address, fund, and get out of the way while more knowledgeable leaders deal with the crisis.
4. Allowing partisan politics and egos to usurp the best actions for the entire country.

It seems there has not been any authentic leadership beyond words in either the Executive or Legislative branches that addresses the very serious and growing problems occasioned by the rise of climate change issues. Because the government branches have repeatedly demonstrated that they are impotent in addressing the climate change problems, it is imperative that a different organizational structure be given the authority to do so.

This action would require that the Executive and Legislative Branches act in the very best interests of the country by delegating the responsibility of finding solutions to the climate /change problems to a separate agency. Funds would have to be allocated for the work of this organization and for the costly actions associated with implementing the solutions that are developed.

THE SMITHSONIAN
AND THE
WORLD HEALTH ORGANIZATION

The Smithsonian as an institution is uniquely equipped for undertaking such a leadership position in seeking scientific solutions to the problems associated with climate change. In fact, Lonnie G. Branch III, Smithsonian Secretary, has addressed this very subject in the November 2021 issue of the <u>Smithsonian</u>. As he points out, the Smithsonian is an interdisciplinary research institution, a center of education and learning, and a trusted source of information.

There is another critical element in having the Smithsonian act in this leadership capacity. Climate change is not just an American crisis, and there is no way that the fact that climate change is a worldwide crisis can be ignored.

The Smithsonian is recognized worldwide for its prestigious accomplishments with a worldwide focus. If the Smithsonian were to invite the most outstanding museum or research center in each country, it would be expected that each would be more than willing to participate in such a planet-wide endeavor.

Working groups, established by disaster type and composed of the leading experts in each type, should be established. A coordinating committee would be able to identify interactive elements within and between types and social disorder behaviors. These groups would provide a powerful mechanism for identifying, researching, and recommending how each disaster type's effects could be lessened.

The mission of such an enterprise would be at least three-fold. First, develop specific strategies for addressing the major climate change problems in each country.

Second, research the relationships between natural disasters and social disorders, emphasizing predicting outbreaks of both.

Third, identify the priority needs of each country or region for initial focus.

These activities require full-time and more effective attention in their efforts. Political efforts could not afford to devote full time to such activities. This is another critical reason for having an institution like the Smithsonian lead the effort. The time available to develop, plan, and implement such an effort is much shorter than most people realize. Action must be taken immediately.

WORLD HEALTH ORGANIZATION

According to the World Economic Forum, The World Health Organization is a specialized agency of the United Nations. It was inaugurated following the second world war on 7 April 1948 – a date now celebrated as World Health Day. The organization grew out of the International Sanitary Conferences, which convened between 1851 and 1938 to combat diseases such as cholera, yellow fever, and bubonic plague. Its self-proclaimed mission is the "attainment by all peoples of the highest possible level of health".

It is probably most recognized for the work it does in identifying and collecting and analyzing data on physical illnesses. It The World Health Organization is a specialized agency of the United Nations. It was inaugurated following the second world war on 7 April 1948 – a date now celebrated as World Health Day. The organization grew out of the International Sanitary Conferences, which convened between 1851 and 1938 to combat diseases such as cholera, yellow fever, and bubonic plague. Its self-proclaimed mission is the "attainment by all peoples of the highest possible level of health".

It employs 7,000 staff across six regional offices and 150 field offices. They are well trained in data collection and analytical procedures. It does not take much imagination to visualize these same individuals collecting data on social disorder events. Working in conjunction with the Smithsonian the collaboration of the data and its analysis should yield important insights and understandings that are currently unavailable.

CHAPTER 8

PROBLEMS AND CONCLUSIONS

It should be patently clear that not all cases of personal or social disorder or anti-social disorder can be attributed to natural disasters or even a pandemic. The overall data are clear in the trends suggested by the explosion of disasters and the growth of social disorders at the same time.

The extreme uncertainty of the climate crisis—as proven by the fact that even the best predictions failed to account for the worst of the effects—has its own unsettling effect.

"I think the fact that it's kind of happening faster and in a different way than we anticipated just exaggerates that sense of kind of confusion and loss of kind of intellectual stability and that leads to things like climate grief,", according to Susan Clayton, a professor of psychology and environmental studies at the College of Wooster.

Part of the reason it's been so hard to predict these effects in the first place is that they are "complicated, non-linear processes," as Kalmus calls them. Scientists have to account for hundreds of variables, which means predictions are often far from perfect. Models for the melting of ice sheets in the Arctic, for example, are actually more optimistic than what's currently happening in places like Greenland and Antarctica, because those models haven't taken into account the other processes that could accelerate melting (water can creep in under the ice sheets, causing them to slip off into the ocean more quickly, for example). "The models, in this case, have proven overly conservative, not including some important real-world processes," Michael Mann, a prominent climate scientist and the director of the Earth System Science Center at Pennsylvania State University, said about the ice sheet predictions.

In other words, even as we watch the effects already happening, we still have to contend with how they will multiply and exacerbate one another. "We have a lot to learn about specifics about how climate breakdown and how it's going to affect civilization," Kalmus added. "I think there's still a lot we don't know there."

It must be noted that many countries, perhaps most, have been preoccupied with the current challenges facing them and have not addressed climate change effects as an issue that must be faced directly and currently. For example, the COP26 meeting, the 26th annual UN climate change conference held in Glasgow, Scotland on Oct. 2021 resulted in promises of which there have been many during the past years. Indeed, in 26 years, some significant, concrete advances could have been made. In effect, despite all the data and warnings from the scientific and activist communities, governments have essentially done nothing during the past 26 years except make promises for the future

COP26 literally developed into a war of words between

the UN and activists. Standing before scores of other youth activists, Greta Thunberg did not mince words while offering her thoughts on the global climate summit in Glasgow. She emphatically declared the gathering of world leaders and scientists to be a "failure," "PR event," and "a global north green wash festival."

Climate activist Greta Thunberg spoke at the "Fridays For Future" climate rally during COP26 in Glasgow

The Swedish teen activist and thousands of protestors descended on the city to participate in a youth-led climate strike. The demonstration was organized by Fridays For Future Scotland, the Scottish branch of the international youth movement founded by Thunberg in 2018 — when she began cutting class solo in protest, hoping to spur action from her own politicians in Stockholm.

The gathering of youths — who have been vocal in their demands for urgent action on a global scale — highlighted a generational divide at the COP26 United Nations climate summit. Those participating in the conference vowed progress and projected optimism on the climate initiatives being discussed. The demonstrators outside expressed frustration, believing the measures were not going far enough to address the planet's warming.

"It is not a secret that COP26 is a failure," said Thunberg, who headlined the event. "It should be obvious that we cannot solve the crisis with the same methods that got us into it in the first place."

- Increasing numbers of disasters, especially high-intensity ones can exact a cumulative drain on an individual's emotional, financial, social, and personal resources.

- A nationwide epidemic, or a multi-state natural disaster, can drain the resources of the individuals affected and also the states involved.
- There is a statistical and correlational relationship between the advent of disasters and a rise in personal, social, and anti-social behaviors. What is needed are more exact data of critical variables that can be used to:

  a. Predict disasters and their likely behavior, and
  b. Predict from these disaster variables the potential social and anti-social behaviors that may be expected.

- The need for planning in a more comprehensive and inclusive manner is acute.
- A nationwide cadre of educational and trained personnel is needed.

In addition to efforts in America, there needs to be a planet-wide awareness of the exacting toll climate change has already extracted from countries around the world. Unless a planet-wide perspective is developed and plans put in place to protect the planet, lesser efforts will probably not be enough to save us.

A significant first step in better understanding and predicting disasters and their effects is classifying them according to their scope, intensity, and especially the impact they leave behind. Several agencies have developed categories for categorizing several types of disasters. For example, there is the Saffir-Simson Wind Scale which provides four categories of hurricanes dependent on wind speed and types of expected damage for each. Standard agreement about categories and criteria is absolutely essential for planning and implementation efforts.

Needed Research

1. Post-hoc analyses to reveal which natural disasters, their frequency, and intensity, seem to be (1) associated with specific social disorders and (2) the number of social disorder outbreaks.
2. Need for baseline numbers from past years for ascertaining changes. This will require agreement on how to compile the data and methods for comparing.
3. Agreement on what equations will be used for predicting effects.
4. In addition to developing research programs to explore natural disasters, research is badly needed in the area of social disorders.

    a. Are they related to the frequency, intensity, and/ or other natural disaster variables?
    b. What are the underlying causes prompting behavior of a disordered type? Do they tend to manifest themselves more frequently or violently during times of natural disasters?

Perhaps the most important element of all is developing a conceptual framework of non-linear dimensions of the interactions of the systems. It is the nature of the interactions that are most important for understanding and predicting future behavior.

The Growing Influence of Human Activities

This type of thinking should also be extended to other levels of interactions. For example. The World Trade Organization is an international organization established to supervise and liberalize world trade. It has issued a warning of a global food crisis. Much of this crisis could be brought about by climate change effects.

However, it is exacerbated by the recent actions of Russia and China. The planet and many countries are facing famine levels of food insecurity. Russia is holding up vast quantities of grain in Ukraine primarily destined for Africa.

China has been making significant advances in Africa in a number of areas. It has also bought thousands of acres of farmland in America. They could easily intensify famine conditions existing around the planet. The actions of these two countries have significant potential for interacting in ways that would not be beneficial for the rest of the world.

Neither country has made a secret of its desire to significantly increase its land holdings, Russia through war and holding hostile larges shipments of grain, and China through financial means. The Chinese Communist Party (CCP) is continuing its U.S. agricultural takeover, buying hundreds of thousands of arable acres across the nation. The purchase of U.S. land is part of the CCP's food security initiative, posing a significant threat to food and national security for the American public.

The interaction of these systems centered around increases in land, and the real possibility of using food staples as hostages pose a troubling and forthcoming set of policy decisions that would be better made earlier than later The critical element is understanding that their actions interact with climate change-related disasters. These system interactions are difficult to unravel and ameliorate.

CONCLUSIONS

There is any number of conclusions that can be inferred from the current and forthcoming growth of the dangers and perils associated with climate change and its influence on natural disasters and social violence. The efforts to ameliorate the current effects of natural disasters are disconnected and do not take into account;

- The interrelationship among various types of disasters,
- The growing threat of even more dangerous disasters,
- The lack of understanding of the connections between natural disasters and social disorder and violence,
- The potential for human influence on specific types of disasters,
- The lack of a coordinated, planet-wide effort with sufficient funding to address the problems on a preventative basis,

- The effective involvement of the scientific community to research and develop the means necessary for protecting the planet, and
- Developing a worldwide perspective and understanding of the perilous condition the planet is in.

These understandings and perspectives need to be developed and reinforced across the planet so a majority of individuals will be willing to make the sacrifices necessary to achieve the level of protection needed. The future of the planet depends on the extent to which these are achieved.

REFERENCES

Borunda, Alejandra, A Shady Divide, July, 2021, National Geographic, 66-84.

Branch, Lonnie, How the Smithsonian Grapples with Climate Change, Smithsonian, November, 2021

Cadena, Fernando. Speaking as head of the Mexican ranching company Carnes Ribe.

Casassa, Gino, South America's glaciers may have a bigger problem than climate change. Bloomberg News | August 14, 2019

Clayton, Susan, (2020). Mental Health on a Changing Planet. https://islandpress.org/books/planetary-health

CDC, 2007, Report Epidemic After Disasters. (Volume 13, No.1-January)

Department of Homeland Security, U.S. Government, Washington, D.C,

Disaster Recovery Reform Act of 2018 (DRRA, Division D of P.L. 115-254)

Dodds, Kieran, Marvels Revealed by the Thaw, November 2021, National Geographic, 76-79.

Editorial Board, Opinion: Drug trafficking and an assassination have deepened Haiti's chaos, Washington Post, December 14, 2021.

Gallup Report, State of the Global Work Place, 2021.

Gardiner, Beth, April 2021, National Geographic, 41-78).

Gibbens, Sarah, Tracking the Melt, September, 2021, National Geographic, 86-93.

Green, Gloria, Feb. 19, 2021 — Deputy Under Secretary for Farm Production and Conservation (FPAC).

Guterres, Antonio. Fall, 2021, COP26 Conference, Gaslow, Scotland.

Jayeshe, Earthquakes, Categories and Types. Ayaearthquakes. Weebly.com 2012

Jyothi, Abdu, https://www.wired.com/story/solar-storm-internet-apocalypse-undersea-cables. March, sosa.

Kelman, Llan, writing in the Washington Post 2021

Kalmus, Peter, (2021). What needs to happen to climate. Los Angeles Times, Nov. 16.

Leffer, L. (June 21, 2022). Stifling: Extreme heat hammers the US. https,Gizmoo.com

Mann, M The New Climate War. 2021. www. Amazon.com.

Murphy, K. INN Daily Newsletter, March 21, 2018.

National Geographic, In America's Hunger Crisis, Charities are a Lifeline, August, 2021, 86-109.

Nebehay, Stephanie, writing for Reuters in the Oct. 12, 2020 issue of Environment.

Nickal, Rod & Polansek, Tom. Drought forces North American ranchers to sell their future. Reported Sept. 3, 2021, Reuters.

Our World in Data is a scientific online publication that focuses on large global problems.

Perillat, Brian, Manager and Senior Analyst, CanFax, based in Calgary, Alberta.

Pilson, Gaby, Outfornia, Wipedia, 2021

Reilly, David, The Pace of Instructional Presentation, Non-Linear Systems, Effectiveness of Cognitive Processing, and Needed Research in the Use of Technology of Instruction. 1998, 25(3), Journal of Instructional Psychology.

Reilly, David. To be published, 2022, <u>Beware! The Cascading has Arrived</u>. Austin Macauley.

Royte, Elizabeth, July, 2021, <u>National Geographic,</u> 40-65.

Sandy Recovery Improvement Act of 2013 (SRIA, Division B of P.L. 113-2)

Serrata, Josie, 2021, https://www.vitadox.com

Schultz, Kathryn, 2015, The Really Big One, <u>The New Yorker,</u> July 20.

Scales, Helen, An Icy World in Meltdown, November, 2021, <u>National Geographic</u>, 101-121

Smith, Adam, (NCEI's) U.S. Billion-dollar Weather and Climate Disasters. NOAA, January 8, 2021.

Specktor, Brandon (2021) MSN News, SIGCOMM Conference.

Spratling, Cassandra, Oct. 2021<u>, National Geographic</u>, 86-109. cbsnews-intelligence-matters-podcast-horizontal-620x350. jpg© Credit: CBSNews cbsnews-intelligence-matters-podcast-horizontal-620x350.jpg

Thunberg, Greta, 2021, Nov. 12. "Fridays For Future" COP26, Glasgow, Scotland.

Thewashingtonstandard.com/china-continues-to-buy-us-farm-land-hr4356-is-a-feeble-attempt-to-prohibit-it/

Turrentine, Jeff, Jan. 2019. <u>Climate Change Is Already Driving Mass Migration Around the Globe, on Earth, Culture & Politics.</u>

Von Massow, Mike, University of Guelph; Ontario, Canada.

Wallace, Tim, Ashley Wu, and Jugal K. Patel, How Haiti Was Devastated by Two Natural Disasters in Three Days. <u>NY Times</u>. Aug. 18, 2021
    www.dhs.gov/natural-disasters
    www. Loving systems. Com
    www.nbcnews.com › science › science-newsWorldwide(2020
    www.nbcwashington.com/weather, tidal-flooding-hits-dc-area/2857840October, 29. 2021.
    www.drought.gov › data-maps-tools › us-drought-monitor US Drought Monitor.
    <u>www.usgs.gov</u>. 7.2 Earthquake hits Haiti (August, 14, 2021.
    <u>www.Wikipedia.org</u>

(WTO) | History & Facts | Britannicahttps://www.britannica.com › ... › International Relations